SUPERCARS

BUGATTI

Ryan Smith

AV2
www.av2books.com

Step 1
Go to **www.av2books.com**

Step 2
Enter this unique code

QOBVYD95T

Step 3
Explore your interactive eBook!

AV2 is optimized for use on any device

Your interactive eBook comes with...

Contents
Browse a live contents page to easily navigate through resources

Audio
Listen to sections of the book read aloud

Videos
Watch informative video clips

Weblinks
Gain additional information for research

Try This!
Complete activities and hands-on experiments

Key Words
Study vocabulary, and complete a matching word activity

Quizzes
Test your knowledge

Slideshows
View images and captions

... and much, much more!

SUPERCARS

BUGATTI

CONTENTS

BUG

ATTI

BUGATTI SUPERCARS

Supercars are a special class of car. Some cars might be fast, **luxurious**, or rare, but a supercar is all three and much more. A supercar often has a big engine with lots of **horsepower**. All parts of a supercar are designed to look elegant and fast. Only so many supercars are made each year because so much work goes into each car. All the features that make supercars special also make them cost hundreds of thousands of dollars.

Since 1909, Bugatti has used its cars to blend art and **performance**. Each car is different from the previous one. Bugatti only builds a certain number of each **model**. Today's Bugattis are some of the fastest cars on the road. Some are so powerful and luxurious that they are considered **hypercars**.

The average **Bugatti** is up to **10 times more expensive** than the average **Ferrari**.

Customers often have to wait up to **3 years** to buy a **Bugatti**.

ETTORE BUGATTI

"Nothing is too expensive, nothing is too beautiful." -Ettore Bugatti

Ettore Bugatti first worked for a company that built motorized tricycles. He designed new models for the company. Ettore got his first job in the car industry in 1902. The company was not as interested as Ettore was in race cars. Ettore started to design cars on his own. In 1909, he started the Bugatti car company in France. The company started building and racing its cars right away.

Ettore would often test drive the cars his company made.

MAP OF FRANCE

The largest collection of Bugattis is at the Cité de l'Automobile National Museum in Mulhouse, France.

THE MACARON

Ettore's father, Carlo Bugatti, was a famous artist in Milan, Italy. Ettore asked his father to create a logo for the Bugatti company. Carlo designed a logo that matched the power and elegance of his son's cars. The oval logo has never changed since it was first unveiled in 1909.

Carlo was known for the furniture, jewelry, and musical instruments he made.

BUGATTI LOGO

The red background represents passion and power.

Ettore Bugatti's initials sit above the family name.

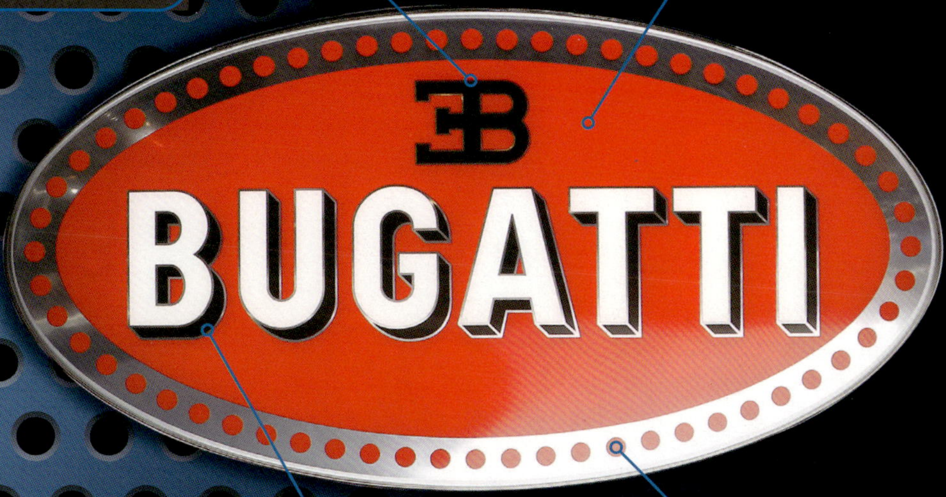

The family name is outlined in black to help it stand out.

The 60 red dots are thought to represent either pearls or the red safety wires used on a car's engine.

BUGATTI THROUGH HISTORY

Many members of the Bugatti family were talented artists. Their passion for art inspired the elegance of the company's cars. Today, Bugatti cars are known for their artistic beauty and powerful performance.

1910

The Bugatti company builds its first car, the Type 10.

1929

Bugatti wins the Monaco **Grand Prix** for the first time.

1982

Cité de l'Automobile National Museum opens. The cars it showcases include more than 120 Bugattis.

Bugatti celebrates its 110th anniversary by launching the **exclusive** Bugatti La Voiture Noire and Bugatti Centodieci models.

Volkswagen AG buys the rights to the Bugatti brand.

1998

2005

2019

The construction of the Bugatti factory, Atelier, is completed.

FAMOUS BUGATTIS

Perhaps the best-known Bugatti is a missing Type 57 Atlantic Coupe. Four of these cars were built before **World War II**. One black Atlantic was used as a **show car** by the factory. It disappeared around the beginning of the war. The car may have been destroyed during World War II. It may also still be out there somewhere, waiting to be discovered.

The missing Atlantic Coupe would be worth $113 million if it were found.

Ralph Lauren's car collection includes one of the remaining Atlantic Coupes. He had it painted black.

One Atlantic Coupe had to be completely rebuilt after it was hit by a train in 1955.

With a starting price of more than $1 million per car, very few people can afford to buy a Bugatti. Famous actors and athletes such as Tom Cruise and Tom Brady have purchased Bugattis. Many people who buy Bugattis tend to be car collectors and own more than one. Famous celebrities such as Ralph Lauren and Jay Leno have Bugattis in their collections.

Tom Cruise drove his Bugatti Veyron to the premiere of *Mission Impossible III* in 2006.

AT THE RACES

Bugatti found success in races early in its history. In 1911, the Type 13 came in second in the French Grand Prix. Bugatti continued to improve on its car designs. From 1925 to 1939, Bugatti came first several times in major races such as Targa Florio, Monaco, and Le Mans.

Today, Bugatti honors its racing tradition by improving the performance of its cars. In 2019, the Bugatti Chiron became the first supercar to go faster than 300 miles per hour (482.8 kilometers per hour).

Renowned race car driver Louis Chiron raced in Bugattis from 1925 to 1932.

Bugatti has tried out many body shapes on its race cars over the years.

The **Chiron** reached a **top speed** of **304.8 mph** **(490.5 km/h).**

Famous race car driver Pierre Veyron won races in Bugattis such as the Type 51.

In **2013**, the **Bugatti Veyron 16.4 Grand Sport** set a **speed record** of **254 mph** **(408.8 km/h).**

The Bugatti Chiron was named in honor of Louis Chiron.

HOW IT'S MADE

Bugattis are made in a factory in Molsheim, France. The Bugatti factory is located behind the Bugatti family **estate**. The factory is called Atelier. *Atelier* means "the studio" in French. Atelier is treated more like an art studio than a car factory. The building is shaped like the Bugatti logo. Each Bugatti is built by hand and made **unique** for its buyer.

About 20 people work on each Bugatti.

Car designers work to bring the customer's vision to life.

Fewer than 100 Bugattis are built **every year.**

A **Chiron** is made up of **more than 1,800** parts.

Each Bugatti is tested throughout production.

The final inspection takes 6 hours.

TODAY'S LINEUP

Bugatti cars are special because they are exclusive. When the Chiron was launched, Bugatti announced it would only build 500 of them. By early 2020, more than 400 Chirons had been sold, and 250 of the 500 had been built.

Here are some of the Bugattis on the road today.

Bugatti Veyron 16.4

Engine: **W16**

Maximum Horsepower: **1,001**

0–60 mph (0–100 km/h): **2.5 seconds**

Starting Price: **$1,700,000**

Bugatti Veyron 16.4 Grand Sport Vitesse

Engine: **W16**

Maximum Horsepower: **1,200**

0–60 mph (0–100 km/h): **2.6 seconds**

Starting Price: **$2,500,000**

Bugatti Chiron

Engine: **W16**

Maximum Horsepower: **1,500**

0–60 mph (0–100 km/h): **2.3 seconds**

Starting Price: **$2,998,000**

Bugatti Chiron Super Sport 300+

Engine: **W16**

Maximum Horsepower: **1,600**

0–60 mph (0–100 km/h): **2.3 seconds**

Starting Price: **$3,890,000**

Bugatti DIVO

Engine: **W16**

Maximum Horsepower: **1,500**

0–60 mph (0–100 km/h): **2.4 seconds**

Starting Price: **$5,800,000**

TOMORROW'S BUGATTI

Bugatti's plan for the future is to continue making cars that are also works of art. For now, Bugatti is taking orders for its limited-edition models. The Centodieci and the La Voiture Noire are designed as tributes to 110 years of Bugatti cars.

The Centodieci is inspired by the Bugatti EB110. The EB110 helped revive the Bugatti name in the 1990s.

The La Voiture Noire is a tribute to the Bugatti that went missing from the factory during World War II. The La Voiture Noire is the most expensive new car ever sold, costing $19 million.

The EB110 was unveiled on Ettore Bugatti's 110th birthday.

The EB110 has a top speed of 218 mph (351 km/h).

Only 10 of the Centodieci will be built.

Only one La Voiture Noire has been built.

BUGATTI QUIZ

1 How many Bugattis are built in a year?

2 When did Ettore Bugatti get his first job with a car company?

3 How many times has the Bugatti logo changed?

4 What was the name of the first car the Bugatti company produced?

5 Which Bugatti went missing during World War II?

6 Which Bugatti was the first supercar to go faster than 300 mph (482.8 km/h)?

7 What does *Atelier* mean in French?

8 How many Bugatti Chirons does Bugatti plan to build?

9 What kind of engine does Bugatti use in the Chiron?

10 How much did it cost to buy the La Voiture Noire?

ANSWERS
1 Fewer than 100 **2** 1902 **3** It has never changed **4** The Type 10 **5** A black Type 57 Atlantic Coupe **6** The Bugatti Chiron **7** "The studio" **8** 500 **9** W16 **10** $19 million

KEY WORDS

estate: a large house on a large piece of land owned by one person or family

exclusive: limited in number

Grand Prix: a series of high-level races

horsepower: the equivalent power that is produced by one horse pulling

hypercars: cars even more powerful, luxurious, and rare than supercars

luxurious: something that is pleasing and comfortable

model: a particular car design made by a company

performance: how well a car accelerates and turns

show car: a car put on display to help sell its model or brand

unique: when something is different from other things of its type

World War II: a war that was fought from 1939 to 1945

INDEX

Get the best of both worlds.

AV2 bridges the gap between print and digital.

The expandable resources toolbar enables quick access to content including **videos**, **audio**, **activities**, **weblinks**, **slideshows**, **quizzes**, and **key words**.

Animated videos make static images come alive.

Resource icons on each page help readers to further **explore key concepts**.

Published by AV2
14 Penn Plaza, 9th Floor
New York, NY 10122
Website: www.av2books.com

Library of Congress Cataloging-in-Publication Data

Names: Smith, Ryan, author.
Title: Bugatti / Ryan Smith.
Description: New York, NY : AV2, [2021] | Series: Supercars | Includes index. | Audience: Ages 8-12. | Audience: Grades 4-6.
Identifiers: LCCN 2020016892 (print) | LCCN 2020016893 (ebook) | ISBN 9781791125875 (library binding) | ISBN 9781791125882 (paperback) | ISBN 9781791125899 | ISBN 9781791125905
Subjects: LCSH: Chiron automobile--Juvenile literature.
Classification: LCC TL215.B82 S65 2021 (print) | LCC TL215.B82 (ebook) | DDC 629.222--dc23
LC record available at https://lccn.loc.gov/2020016892
LC ebook record available at https://lccn.loc.gov/2020016893

Printed in Guangzhou, China
1 2 3 4 5 6 7 8 9 0 24 23 22 21 20

062020
101119

Art Director: Terry Paulhus Project Coordinator: Ryan Smith

The publisher acknowledges Alamy, Getty Images, Shutterstock, and Wikimedia as its primary image suppliers for this title.